D1441988

DOLLARS AND SENSE
A GUIDE TO FINANCIAL LITERACY ™

The Stock Market

CHARLES NORTH AND
CHARLES CAES

rosen publishing's
rosen
central®

NEW YORK

Published in 2012 by The Rosen Publishing Group, Inc.
29 East 21st Street, New York, NY 10010

First Edition

Library of Congress Cataloging-in-Publication Data

North, Charles.
The stock market/Charles North, Charles Caes.
    p. cm. — (Dollars and sense: a guide to financial literacy)
Includes index.
ISBN 978-1-4488-4717-4 (library binding) —
ISBN 978-1-4488-4723-5 (pbk.) —
ISBN 978-1-4488-4755-6 (6-pack)
1. Stock exchanges–Juvenile literature. 2. Finance, Personal—Juvenile literature.
I. Caes, Charles J. II. Title. III. Series.
HG4553.N67 2012
332.64'2—dc22

                                                          2011008260

Manufactured in the United States of America

CPSIA Compliance Information: Batch #S11YA: For further information, contact Rosen Publishing, New York, New York, at 1-800-237-9932.

CONTENTS

When people refer to the "stock market," they are actually referring to many organizations around the world that provide the means to buy and sell stock in public corporations. A public corporation is one that is not privately owned and in which the general public, including you and me, have the right and opportunity to invest. One reason why large corporations welcome investors is because it gives them the capital, or money, to run the business from day to day.

More likely than not, when you buy stock it will be through a broker, who, in turn, trades for you on stock exchanges. So when you purchase stock, you rarely buy it directly from the company that issued it. You usually buy it from other investors like yourself.

When a corporation like Microsoft or McDonald's issues new securities, it sells them directly to investment bankers. These investment bankers are usually giant brokerage firms, such as Goldman Sachs and Citigroup.

A broker or brokerage is an intermediary—someone in between—the seller and the purchaser of a security. In this case, what is being sold are shares of stock. The brokers help create the secondary markets through which you and I can trade stocks. The term "secondary market" means that the stocks are no longer purchased from the corporation that issued them. Now they are purchased from exchanges or businesses providing electronically linked facilities all around the world.

Most buying and selling of stock takes place in the secondary markets. But there are plans by which you can buy stock directly from a company. In fact, your parents may work for a company that has a stock-purchase plan that allows them to have money taken from their paychecks every week in order to buy the company's stock.

CHAPTER **ONE**

A LOOK AT THE STOCK MARKET

You probably like to go with your mom and dad to shopping malls. And why not? They are convenient marketplaces where many different types of stores can be found in the same location. Clothing stores! Candy stores! Bakeries! Toy stores! Even places to sit down and eat, like McDonald's!

When people want to invest in a corporation, they go to another kind of marketplace. It is called the stock market. A stock market is just like a great mall, only instead of many stores, it has lists of companies in which people, including

The most recognizable stock exchange in the United States is the New York Stock Exchange. Billions of stock transactions happen on the floor of the NYSE every day.

you, can invest: McDonald's, Hershey's, Kmart, IBM, and thousands of other companies around the world.

What does it mean to "invest in a company"? It means purchasing shares of stock in that corporation. Investors do so in hopes of selling that stock later for more than they paid for it. If they can sell their ownership in a corporation like McDonald's for $10,000 when they paid only $5,000 for that ownership, they will make a profit of $5,000 ($10,000 - $5,000 = $5,000). This is one form of what is called speculation in the stock market. Basically, speculation means to invest in a stock in the hopes of profiting from a change in its selling price.

That is not unlike what the owners of those stores in the mall do. They buy clothing or other goods from the people who make them and then try and sell them to you for more money than they paid for them.

THE DOW JONES INDUSTRIAL AVERAGE

Business news reports often state that "the Dow was up today" or "the Dow Jones took a hit today." The Dow Jones Industrial Average is a kind of index, or reference point, that gives an overall sense of how the stock market is doing. There is no way to quickly report the results of every company during the day, so the Dow is an average of the thirty most widely held and largest companies in the United States. The Dow does not indicate how every company that is traded on the New York Stock Exchange (NYSE) performed. It is simply an average of some of the biggest of them.

Instead of clothing or toys or cars or other goods, stock investors buy "into" corporations such as McDonald's or the Ford Motor Company. That means they buy a part of the corporation. They become one of the owners of the corporation. Their ownership in any of these corporations will be represented by shares of stock. If a corporation issues one million shares of stock and an investor owns ten thousand shares, then that investor owns 1 percent of the company (10,000/1,000,000 = .01).

The Exchanges: Where Stock Is Traded

Stock exchanges are where stock is traded. Stock exchanges are auction markets because the prices of the corporate stocks they list are determined solely by supply and demand. This means that if there are not enough shares of stock in a particular company for all the people who want to buy some, the price of the stock will most likely go up. If there are too many shares of stock and not enough people to buy them all, then the price of the stock will probably go down. The price of the stock is not fixed. The buy offer is called the bid price, and the sell offer is called the asking price. In essence, the stock is being auctioned off.

There are many stock exchanges around the world—more than 150. Large and wealthy countries have many exchanges. The United States has several, including the New York Stock Exchange. These alone account for billions of shares of stock being traded almost every day.

In the United States, the term "Wall Street" is often used in a general way to refer to the stock market. That is because the Federal Reserve, the American Stock Exchange, the New York Stock Exchange, the New York Mercantile Exchange, and many brokerage firms are located on Wall Street in lower Manhattan in New York City.

While New York may be the first place one thinks of when it comes to stock exchanges, there are exchanges in most major cities, such as Hong Kong.

Each exchange has different sets of requirements for companies that want to have their stocks listed for sale to the public. These requirements include, among other things:

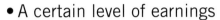

- A certain level of earnings
- A certain amount of stock available for the public to buy
- A certain number of stockholders
- A certain amount of financial stability
- A certain amount of growth potential

Some of the foreign exchanges that you may have heard about are the London Stock Exchange, the Paris Bourse, and the Montreal Stock Exchange. Not all foreign countries have stock exchanges, but most do, including Argentina, Australia, Hong Kong, Japan, India, Italy, the Netherlands, New Zealand, Norway, Spain, and Venezuela—to name just a few.

Though not the only stock exchange, the New York Stock Exchange is the largest in the world in terms of market value. It is second largest in terms of volume of transactions, behind the National Association of Securities Dealers Automated Quotations (NASDAQ), also based in New York. Each year, trillions of dollars of stock trade through the NYSE exchange on four trading room floors. Brokers do the buying and selling at the direction of their customers who place orders.

The NASDAQ, founded in 1971, is important for both brokers and investors. It is an electronic stock exchange where brokers can buy and sell stocks via computer. About thirty-eight thousand companies trade their securities through the NASDAQ exchange. It has more trading volume per hour than any other exchange in the world.

The NASDAQ is an index as well as a stock exchange. A stock index is a measurement of the performance of a sample collection of companies' stocks, usually the stocks of the largest companies traded in that exchange. When the news reports that "the NASDAQ gained 100 points today," it means the collective value of the stocks chosen for its index went up by that number of points. When the point value of the NASDAQ is reported, a percentage gain or loss is also reported. This is a more important indicator of how the stock market did that day. It may have gained 2 percent or lost 1.5 percent of its cumulative value (total worth of the stock of the companies in the index). These numbers let investors know if the stock market as a whole is gaining or losing value, since the companies in the index are taken to be representative of the larger economy.

The Standard and Poor's 500, or simply the S&P 500, is another index for reporting stock averages. It is an index of five hundred companies, the largest ones holding a greater weight on the index than the smaller ones.

The Different Kinds of Stock

When you buy stock in a corporation, you receive a certificate representing the amount of shares you have purchased. If you buy 100 shares of stock in McDonald's, for example, then you will receive a stock certificate representing a value of 100

Shares of nearly all major corporations are traded on the stock exchange. The most established companies, such as McDonald's, are usually the safest investments.

shares. You always have the option of instructing the broker-age firm from which you purchased the stock not to issue you a certificate but to keep an electronic record of your purchase.

Common stock is popular because it gives you the following privileges:

- Protection. If the corporation in which you have invested does poorly or goes out of business, the most money that you can lose is what you paid for shares of stock you own, except in very unusual circumstances.
- Profit sharing. When the corporation earns money (earns a profit), some of that money will be paid directly to you.

Any company, such as Ford Motor Company, that's traded on the stock exchange is partly owned by its shareholders, who have the right to speak directly to its management.

- Liquidity. There is almost always a market for common stock, meaning there is usually someone ready to buy the stock you own if you decide to sell it, though you may not be able to get exactly the price you want for it.

- Voting rights. As a common stockholder, you have the right to help select the top managers and vote on important company business.

Some of the important company issues that you will vote on are:

- Who will be the officers and directors of the corporation
- How much officers and directors will be paid
- Number of shares of stock to be held by company officers and directors
- Changes to the corporation's bylaws (laws under which the corporation must operate)

Some corporations allow preferred stockholders to receive dividends whether or not the corporation has made any money. Dividends are periodic payments a company makes to its shareholders. If the corporation skips a dividend payment, it will be made up to you at a later date. This is called a cumulative feature. Other corporations, however, allow preferred stockholders to receive cash dividends only if the corporation has made money.

Some preferred stocks are callable, which means that the corporation can buy them back on a certain date and at a certain price. This gives the corporation greater flexibility in managing its finances. But you must realize that whether you are a common stockholder or a preferred stockholder, a corporation is never required by law to pay you dividends—unless it actually declares its intention to pay dividends. Preferred stock gives an investor the following advantages:

• Preference. As a preferred stockholder, you get paid dividends before common stockholders.
• Higher dividend rates. While you do not share in profits the way common stockholders do, you will generally receive higher dividends.
• Added protection. If the corporation goes bankrupt (out of business), you will receive its value remains before common stockholders receive their share.

CHAPTER **TWO**

UNDERSTANDING DIVIDENDS AND SPLITS

As mentioned earlier, dividends are payments that a corporation makes to its stockholders. Dividends make stock attractive to investors, and companies use dividends as one way to get you to buy their stock, rather than someone else's. These dividends represent a sharing of a corporation's earnings with its shareholders.

But dividends may not always represent a sharing of corporate earnings. Sometimes a company will not earn profits but will pay dividends anyway. It does this in order to keep a record of continuous payments and keep the stock attractive to buyers. When dividends are not paid from profits, they are based on the growth of the investment that has been made in the company. There are two types of dividends that are paid to shareholders: cash and stock distributions.

Cash Dividends

Cash dividends are payments in money to holders of a corporation's stock. Cash dividends are more popular with

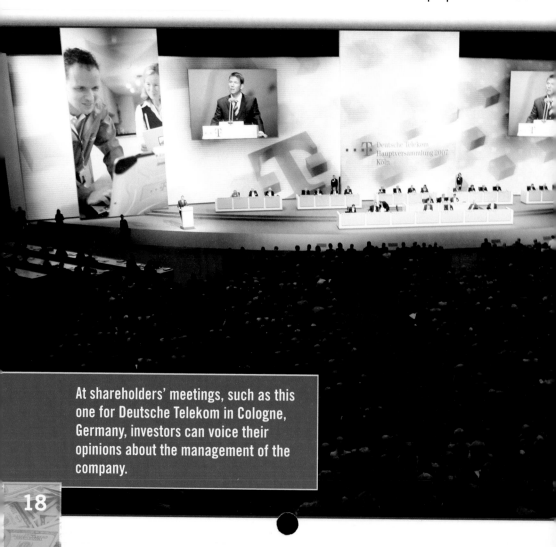

At shareholders' meetings, such as this one for Deutsche Telekom in Cologne, Germany, investors can voice their opinions about the management of the company.

income-oriented investors. If you own 100 shares of common stock and a corporation declares a $1 per share cash dividend, then you will receive $100. If you own 200 shares of stock and a corporation declares a $2 per share dividend, then you will receive $400. It is all a matter of simple arithmetic.

Just remember that a corporation is not legally bound to pay a dividend to its shareholders unless it has actually declared that it will pay a dividend on a specific date. So if

a company paid a $1.50 per share dividend last year, that does not mean it will pay one this year. But if a corporation declares to its stockholders that it will pay a dividend of $1 per share on January 15 or any other date, then it is legally bound to do so.

Dividends may be declared any time a corporation wishes to share its earning with its stockholders. It may pay them every three months, every six months, once a year—as many times as it wishes, but it will rarely pay them more than four times a year except under special circumstances.

These special circumstances include when the corporation has had an exceptionally profitable period, when the corporation is trying to create special interest in its stock, and when the corporation is putting together a strategy to avoid takeover by another company.

A STOCK MARKET GIANT

We can see real-life examples of how the stock market works by examining the fortunes of a few companies throughout their history. One stock market success story can be found in the oil industry. Back in the 1860s, John D. Rockefeller made a fortune building processing plants that refined petroleum. He recognized and anticipated the public demand for oil. The machines of the Industrial Revolution required oil to keep them working. People also used oil in kerosene lamps in their homes. In 1870, Rockefeller formed the Standard Oil Company, which included his refining plants. The supply of oil was great at this time, and new sources of it were being

found all the time. By 1879, the Standard Oil Company controlled 90 percent of the oil market.

In the years to come, Standard Oil grew and changed many times. The company bought more and more oil fields. As far back as 1877, Standard Oil purchased another company, called Vacuum Oil Company, that it thought would help it continue to grow and produce new products. Purchasing or obtaining another company is known as an acquisition. Companies continue to do this today as a means of growing their business, expanding their offerings, gaining an edge over competitors, and offering their shareholders a way to make even more money.

Standard Oil continued to grow during the twentieth century, thanks in large part to the development of fuel-burning cars, trucks, buses, and airplanes. People suddenly needed oil, refined into gasoline, to transport themselves from place to place. There was a great demand for this resource, and shareholders made more and more money as the years went by. The company reacted to the ups and downs of the economy throughout the twentieth century, but it was successful enough to offer shareholders regular dividends and several stock splits.

John D. Rockefeller is considered one of the greatest entrepreneurs in history. He made his fortune by selling shares of his Standard Oil Company to the public.

Stock Dividends

Sometimes a corporation will pay its shareholders in stock, rather than money, when it declares a dividend. If you own 300 shares of stock and a corporation declares a 50 percent stock dividend, then you will receive an additional 150 shares (.50 x 300). If you own 300 shares of stock and a corporation declares a 20 percent stock dividend, you will receive an additional 60 shares of stock (.20 x 300). In the final analysis, only a simple knowledge of arithmetic is needed to understand stock dividends. But they are tricky, so read what follows carefully.

A 50 percent stock dividend may also be expressed as one new share for every two that you own; a 20 percent as one new share for every five that you own; and a 10 percent as one new share for every ten that you own. However, though the number of shares you own has increased after each of the above stock payments, the total value of your shares will remain the same because a stock dividend is simply a bookkeeping game. This means if you have 300 shares worth $3,000 and you receive a 50 percent stock dividend, you will now have 450 shares. But each share is now worth only $6.67 instead of $10! The book value of each share is reduced, and there is a proportionate reduction in the current market value of the shares. The number of shares you own has increased while the total value of those shares has remained the same, which means that the value of each individual share has decreased.

Even though you have no more money than before, you have the potential benefits that owning more shares offers. If you received a cash dividend, you would have to pay taxes on that money. Because you received stock instead, you will not have to pay taxes until you sell that stock, and only if you sell the stock for a profit.

You will also receive more money from dividends that are paid on each share because you now own more shares. Also, because a stock dividend generally (but not definitely) increases the near-future market value of your stock, you will make more money when you sell that stock. As you now have 150 more shares than before, if the stock does indeed go up in price, you stand to make an additional $150 for every $1 increase in the price of the stock. (You will also lose an additional $150 for every $1 that the stock goes down.)

Splits

There is another type of incentive to investors called a stock split. Whereas a stock dividend affects the book value of the stock, the stock split impacts the par value. To understand a stock split, therefore, you must understand the concept of par value.

Par value is the value placed on a share of stock for book-keeping purposes. It has no significance to the actual value of the stock, for the true value of any stock is what someone is willing to pay for it. For example, a stock may have a $1 per share par value, but its market value may be $100 per share, the market value being the stock's listed price on an exchange. Sometimes common stock will be issued without any par value at all. In the case of preferred stock, however, par value has a very specific purpose.

Now, in the case of a stock split, par value is also split, and so is the current market value of the stock. The arithmetic of the stock split explains it all. If you own 100 shares of AT&T and those shares are worth $50 each, then you have $5,000 worth of stock ($50 x 100 shares = $5,000). But if AT&T declares a 2-for-1 stock split, then your 100 shares of stock will become 200 shares. That means the par value will be reduced by half. If the par value is $1 per share, then after the split, it will be 50 cents per share. Also, the current selling price (market price) of the shares will be reduced by half (50 percent) to $25 (from $50).

On the surface, you have not done much better with the stock split than you have with the stock dividend: you have more shares, but each share is worth less. It is much like someone giving you $2 but saying that from now on each one is worth only 50 cents.

Major corporations such as AT&T can grow so large that their shares eventually need to be divided up. This brings down the stock price to make it more attractive to average investors.

Before the split: You own 100 shares at $50 per share = $5,000

After the split: You own 200 shares at $25 per share = $5,000

However, there can be benefits to the investor from a stock split. Before and after the split, you have $5,000 worth of stock. But after the split, you have more shares—twice as many, even if their total value is still only $5,000. If there is a cash dividend associated with stock before it splits, the cash dividend will also be reduced:

Before 2-for-1 split: Dividend = $1.00 per share

After 2-for-1 split: Dividend = $0.50 per share

Sometimes a company will increase the dividend per share when a stock is split. The main purposes of a stock split are to give shareholders a chance to profit more because they have additional shares and to increase investor interest in the stock through the new and lower price. It is anticipated by management that the lower price of

International corporations such as Daimler AG depend on public announcements of new products to bolster their stock prices.

the stock after the split will make it more affordable to the investment community. The more interest in the stock, the greater its price will rise. And as a stockholder, you want the price of your stock to go up in most cases.

The company declaring the stock split benefits in two unique ways. It has a chance to give something to its stockholders without it costing the corporation any more than administrative expenses. And if the stock split results in increased value of the shares, when the company issues more stock, it can issue it at a higher price.

Stock splits may occur in any ratio. You will often hear of 3-for-2 or 3-for-1 splits or even other combinations. Sometimes, corporations will even declare a reverse split. This means that instead of getting 2 shares for every 1 that you own, you get 1 share for every 2 that you own. Whereas you may have owned 100 shares before the 1-for-2 reverse split, you will have only 50 shares afterward.

Before the reserve split: You own 100 shares at $50 per share = $5,000

After the split: You own 50 shares at $100 per share = $5,000

In the case of the reserve split, everything happens in just the opposite way from a regular split. You have half as many shares, but now the market value of each share is doubled (as well as the par value). Dividends, if they are being paid, will also double on each share. Reverse splits may be 1-for-2,

1-for-3, 2-for-3, or in any ratio that the corporation feels to be advantageous.

The reason for reverse splits is to increase the market value of each share because if a stock price is too low, people may be afraid to buy it for fear that the corporation issuing the stock is not doing well. So, the reverse split is a sort of psychological technique.

You will find, however, that reverse splits are very rare. This is because corporations realize that a reverse split might rightly or wrongly be judged as a response to financial difficulties, and stock prices may suffer.

CHAPTER **THREE**

BEHIND THE QUOTES

You can find stock quotes in many places these days: on the Internet, in the business sections of daily newspapers, in the trading sections of financial publications, and even on your smartphone. Internet financial sites will also list stock trades in a similar format, although Internet listings are usually much more detailed. There is no one format. Some quote listings are highly abbreviated; some are greatly expanded in terms of the data they provide. In all cases, however, stock listings are for common stocks unless otherwise indicated. Stock quotations are usually given in fractions of a dollar, usually in the form of decimals.

Stock quotes, whether viewed in daily newspapers or, more commonly today, on the Internet, are categorized under certain headings such as "52-week high" and "close" price.

What It All Means

Reading a stock chart isn't just a matter of understanding numbers. There are several different columns that represent different features of a stock price. Let's look at what the typical columns represent using American Express as an example.

52-Week High

A price of $25.75 might be the highest price at which American Express Preferred A stock has sold in the last 52 weeks. If

31

the stock closed at $26 for the day, the 52-week high would still show $25.75 until the next day's listing. There are a number of different types of preferred stock that a corporation might issue, as discussed earlier. Some are cumulative, some callable, some participating, some convertible, some a combination. They are usually identified by alpha characters (letters of the alphabet).

52-Week Low

A price of $19.87 might be the lowest price at which American Express Preferred A stock has sold in the last 52 weeks. If the stock closed at $18 for the day, the 52-week low would still show $19.87 until the next day's listing.

Stock

In this column, you will find the name of the stock or an abbreviation of its name.

Div.

This amount indicates the total annual dividend the company has declared in the last 52 weeks.

P/E Ratio

This is the price-to-earnings ratio. It is determined by dividing the current price of each share of common stock by the earnings per share. For instance, a P/E ratio of 32 means that the price of the stock is selling at 32 times the earnings of each share.

The price-to-earnings (P/E) ratio is a calculation that gives investors an indication of the health of a company. It compares the company's performance to its stock price.

The P/E ratio is a very general guide that tells investors whether or not a stock is overpriced. But unless you know the stock very well, and know a lot about its marketplace and trading history, the P/E ratio will have very little meaning for you.

However, if you are interested in knowing what the earnings per share actually are, you can find out by dividing the closing price of the stock ($165) by the P/E ratio of 32. Your answer would be $5.16 per share.

Sales 100s

The number you find in this column represents the number of shares that have been traded for the stock. Simply multiply the number given by 100. Thus, if the number given is 9,442, the number of shares traded for American Express common is 942,200 (9,422 x 100); and for the preferred stock it is 57,300 (573 x 100)

High, Low, Last

The values in these columns represent the trading ranges of the stock for the period covered—usually a full trading day.

Change

The number in this column indicates the difference between this day's closing price and the previous trading day's. If no value is given, then there has been no change in the closing prices.

Evaluating the Information

Many new investors believe they can make a decision to buy or sell a stock simply on the information given in stock quotations. But nothing could be further from the truth. Stock quotations simply give a snapshot of a particular stock's recent performance. A great deal of research should be carried out before you make a decision to buy or sell a particular stock.

Professional investors research a wealth of data to come up with their predictions of what a stock will be valued at in the future.

The categories we have just looked at really tell us little about American Express, for example, as a company. It simply tells us what its trading ranges have been for the year and for the day, how many shares were recently traded, and what the dividend and yield might be.

There is much more to know about the stock before it should be purchased or sold.

What are the company's future prospects? Will sales continue to grow? Will profits continue to grow? Will management remain strong and decisive? Will its national and international markets continue to expand? Are there major competitors ready to take away some of its business? Will it continue to pay a dividend?

These are just some of the questions that must be asked. The stock listings (or stock quotes) do not answer these questions. They are simply a scorecard. All that stock listings can do is bring to your attention stocks that you may want to investigate for purchase or sale. They can do no more.

Be smart. Do not buy a stock because of what it did yesterday or over the previous year.

Buy a stock because of what it can do tomorrow and the next day. Buy it for what it will do in the future.

CHAPTER **FOUR**

PROFITS AND LOSSES

Investors enjoy making their money work for them. That means they want to use their money to earn even more money. Some people accomplish this by putting money in a bank where it will grow slowly but relatively safely.

Others prefer to try and make as much money as they can, so they invest it in the stock market—even though there is a chance they can lose it. These people include stock traders and stock investors. Unlike people who put their money in the bank, stock investors and traders are risk takers. And they know that the more money they want to try and make, the greater the risks they will have to take.

Experienced investors know that the stock market will always go through periods of prosperity and periods of slow growth (or even zero or negative growth). The term used for a period of faster growth and prosperity is called a bull market.

The *Charging Bull* statue near the stock exchange in lower Manhattan has become an iconic symbol of Wall Street optimism.

Like a bull, the market charges on, strong and fierce. During a bull market, stock prices rise and investors make a lot of money. Soon, more and more investors see their colleagues making money and decide they want in on the action, too. So they pour more and more money into the stock market, hoping for similarly big returns on their investment.

A period of economic slowdown is called a bear market. It is thought that the term dates back to the time when traders used to sell valuable bearskins. These skins were sold during periods in which traders feared that the prices of goods were falling. They wanted to get as much money for the bearskins as possible while they still could, so they sold at a reduced price. Another explanation for the term "bear market" is that a bear tears its prey with its claws in a downward motion. A bull, on the other hand, goes after its opponent by pushing upward with its horns.

A bull market and a bear market are opposites of each other. The market normally moves slowly from one kind to another. Investors make more money during a bull market, and it is a symbol of a strong economy. In fact, there is a giant bronze statue of a bull prominently situated in the middle of Wall Street, very close to the stock exchange.

MAKING AND LOSING MONEY

It is not easy to find a stock that is going to be profitable, whether you are a regular day trader or a short seller. That is why successful stock investors and stock traders always do a great deal of studying before they pick a stock in which to invest. There is much to learn about the stock market. A lot of research goes into selecting the right stock and deciding whether you should invest in it.

Now it is time to look more deeply into what it is all about. Let's first look at a very simple example of how money is made on an investment.

Buying Long

Suppose that you have a baseball autographed by a famous baseball player. And suppose that you paid $100 for the baseball. Now someone comes along and wants that baseball so badly that he is willing to pay you $200 for it. If you sell it to him, you will make $100. You sold the baseball for $200. You paid $100 for the baseball. Your profit: $100

It is just basic arithmetic. You made $100 because you were smart enough to sell the baseball for more than you paid for it. That's called buying low and selling high. If you paid $200 for the baseball and sold it for only $100, then you would lose $100. Simple subtraction tells you that.

Now let's look at how money is made on a stock investment. Suppose that instead of investing in that baseball, on February 1

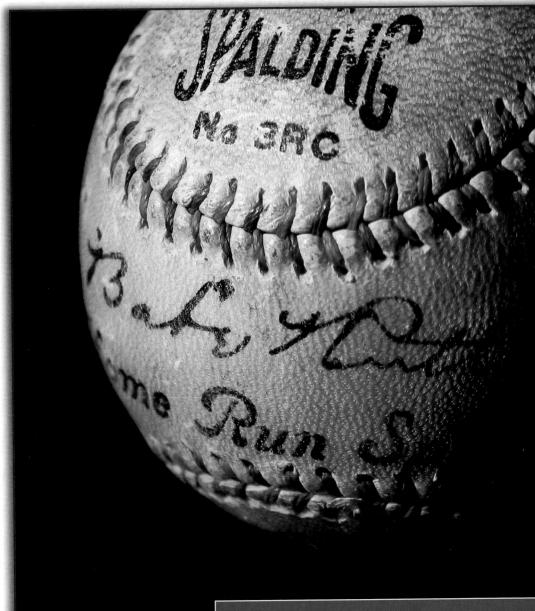

Stocks can be viewed like any other investment, from real estate to collectibles such as sports memorabilia. Their value is determined simply by what people are willing to pay.

you invested $10,000 in shares of stock in PepsiCo, Inc. That is the company that makes Pepsi-Cola. Now suppose that by the following June, business has been so great for PepsiCo that people are willing to pay you $20,000 for your ownership shares in the company. If you decide to sell your holdings, you will make $10,000. You sold your ownership in PepsiCo for $20,000. You bought ownership in PepsiCo for $10,000. Your profit: $10,000.

Why would someone be willing to pay you more for PepsiCo stock than you paid for it? Because she believes business will continue to be good for PepsiCo, and she will be able to sell her stock for even more money at a future date—maybe even one minute after she buys it. Stocks do not always go up, however.

Or she may expect that PepsiCo will continue to increase dividends, and she wants the income from those dividends. There you have it! The formula for making money in the stock market: buy low, sell high. When you buy a stock in the hopes of selling it later at a higher price, you are said to have made a regular way trade. This is also called buying long.

Selling Short

Now you do not have to buy first, then sell, in order to make money. In the stock market you can sell first, then buy. But the formula for success (making a profit) still remains the same: buy low, sell high.

Selling short, or short selling, is a risky and controversial way to make money by betting on the decline of a stock price. One reason why it's so risky is that there is no limit to how high a stock price can rise.

Selling first, then buying back the stock at a later date (or possibly just seconds or minutes later) is called short selling. Buying the stock back is called "covering your position." Investors who engage in short selling are called bears.

Stockbrokers and advisers can help you make the wisest investments based on your long-term goals.

A bear is expecting or hoping the particular stock (or the stock market in general) will go down. A bull, by contrast expects a stock (or the market in general) to go up.

Does this mean that you can sell a stock you do not own? Yes, it most certainly does. Short selling is done when you feel the price of a stock is going to go down and you want to make money when it does so. You see, in the stock market, you can make money when a stock goes up or goes down. For example, consider again PepsiCo stock. Suppose you feel the stock is going to go down $50 per share.

On July 1, you call your broker and tell him you want to sell short 100 shares of the stock at its current price—$100 per share (100 shares x $100 per share = $10,000). The broker borrows the shares from someone else's account—maybe his own—and lends them to you for you to sell. Basically, what you are doing is selling stock that you have borrowed by promising to pay for it later.

You called it right! By August 1, the stock drops by $50 per share and the shares you own are worth only $5,000 (100 shares x $50 = $5,000). So you cover your position by buying back the stock. Your broker now returns the shares to the other person's account. When all the paper shuffling is done, you have made $5,000. Again, it is just simple arithmetic: you bought

100 shares of PepsiCo for $5,000. You sold 100 shares of PepsiCo for $10,000. Your profit: $5,000. It should be noted though that short selling is an extremely risky endeavor. There is greater potential for loss by short selling than there is for traditional investing.

Even though this was a short sale and not a regular way trade, you still stuck to the formula for success: buy low, sell high. The only difference is that you sold first, then bought. But, like most things, buying low and selling high is easy to say and very, very hard to do. You have to be able to predict the way in which the stock is going to move—down for short selling, and up for regular way trades. If the stock goes in the opposite direction than you expect it to go, you will lose money.

CHAPTER **FIVE**

THE STOCK MARKET TODAY

Starting in 2007, the United States entered a difficult period of economic downturn. Economists have compared this severe recession to the Great Depression and the period of time before and after the stock market crash of 1929. While the recession of the late 2000s was not as catastrophic as the Great Depression, there are several similarities that can help people better understand the problems the country faced.

The Real Estate Bubble

During the late 1990s and first half of the 2000s, there was a financial boom in the real estate industry. It became easier

The stock market is connected to all other facets of the economy. The recession of the late 2000s was partly influenced by the decline of the housing industry and mortgage companies such as Freddie Mac.

and easier for people to get a mortgage (a loan to help buy a home). Normally, a mortgage is based on the income of the potential buyers, as well as their ability to repay the loan and their credit history (their track record with paying bills and repaying loans). Banks became more lenient and lent money to people who could not really afford the houses they bought. They didn't have enough income, and often they had poor credit histories.

What's worse, banks lent them money in a way that would cause their payments to go up dramatically—and sometimes unexpectedly for those homeowners who didn't read the fine print—after a few months of relatively low mortgage payments. This often put the monthly house payments beyond the range of the new homeowners. This poor lending practice was ignored by bank regulating authorities, mainly because home prices kept rising along with demand, and banks kept making more and more profits. No one wanted to stop this rising tide of seeming prosperity.

Construction workers enjoyed the boom in new home building. Banks enjoyed the flood of new customers. The stock market enjoyed the rising profits and stock prices of banks, mortgage lenders, and other financial institutions. All of this freewheeling lending and spending and building and buying occurred in part because the government's central bank, the Federal Reserve, was being especially hands-off and not carefully monitoring or regulating the business practices of many lenders and other financial institutions.

Collapse, Defaults, and Foreclosures

There were several factors that may have caused the recession of the late 2000s: buyers in over their heads, reckless lenders, and a lax and inattentive federal government all played a role in creating the housing bubble and the economic crisis that followed its bursting. In late 2008, a stock market crash alerted the country to the trouble that had been brewing for more than a year. Starting on October 6, 2008, the stock market slipped into an eight-day slide and collapse of stock prices. During that same period, the Dow Jones Industrial Average lost 22 percent of its value, or about 2,400 points. The market was very shaky for a period after that, sometimes gaining a little bit of value back only to lose even more over the next couple of days.

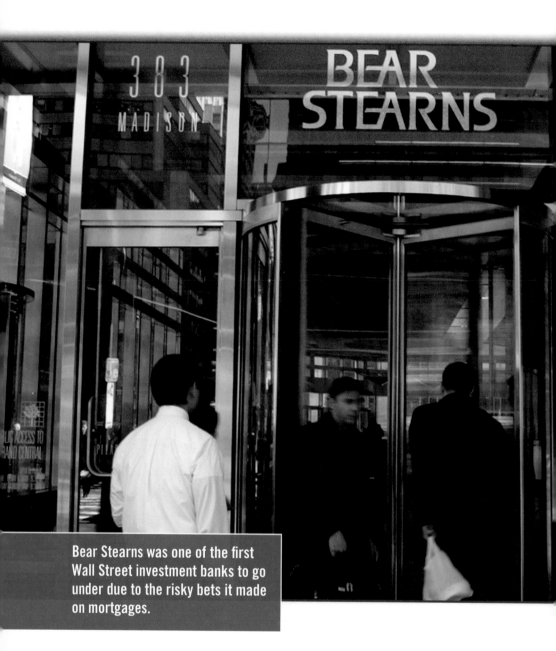

Bear Stearns was one of the first Wall Street investment banks to go under due to the risky bets it made on mortgages.

At the same time that stocks were tanking, many people who were given subprime mortgages were defaulting on their payments and banks were foreclosing on their homes. This meant the people had to move out of their homes, which would

be seized and sold off by the banks that had issued their mortgages. The banks now owned the homes, so they kept any money raised by their sale. Nevertheless, because they had made so many reckless loans that could not be repaid, the banks could no longer cover all of the deposits made by their checking and savings account customers. Banks began to fail, and mortgage companies entered a crisis. In some cases, the government had to step in and use money from the Federal Reserve to cover bank losses. Billions of dollars were lost by these banks and mortgage companies about a month before the stock market crashed.

Meanwhile, more and more people lost their homes. Bank failures left banks unable to lend money to average citizens and companies that needed loans. Consumers stopped spending. Companies were forced to lay off workers. Less money went into the economy. The cycle of economic decline sped up quickly.

How Real Estate Affected the Stock Market

By 2009, most Americans were affected in some manner. Problems now existed in sectors other than the mortgage and

INVESTING AND THE INTERNET

Investing in the stock market has become easier than ever before. The Internet has allowed almost anyone to easily buy any stock they want. The reason is that in the past, investors needed to go through stock brokers to purchase shares in a company. Today, investment Web sites allow the investor to purchase the stock directly, cutting out the middleman stock broker.

While the average person could buy stocks in the past just as today, the Internet has made it much easier—and cheaper—to do so. Investing online cuts out many of the fees traditionally charged by brokers. It also allows investors to buy and sell shares much more quickly with just the press of a button.

Today, online trading firms have made it easier than ever for the average person to own stock. However, it's important that novice investors do their research.

This ease of investing however has both good and bad points. While it can bring prosperity by allowing average working-class people to wisely invest their savings, it also enables abuse. Many online investors participate in a practice called day trading, which is buying and selling stock in the short term, essentially gambling on stock prices rather than investing in companies based on their long-term financial prospects.

Having the tool of online investing requires us to have the knowledge and skills to make wise investments. While it's much easier today to invest and profit from trading stocks, it's just as easy to abuse this power and invest unwisely.

banking industry. Unemployment rose to nearly 10 percent around the country. Although it was not as severe as the downturn of the 1930s, the country was in a financial crisis similar to the one that occurred during the Great Depression.

With a poor economy comes hard times. Small businesses failed because they could not get loans from banks to continue their operations. Larger companies and state and federal governments were forced to cut their budgets to make up for lost revenue.

The financial difficulties of the United States also affected the rest of the world because the United States does so much business with companies around the world. Cutbacks in production and reduced overseas demand for American products translated into fewer exports. The collapse in American consumer spending

On October 3, 2008, President George W. Bush signed the Troubled Asset Relief Program, commonly referred to as TARP, to help the economy out of the subprime mortgage crisis.

translated into fewer imports. As a result, both American and international companies experienced a sales slump and laid off workers, further reducing consumer spending. Economies around the world suffered, and so did the stock prices of

American and foreign companies. The recession that began with the burst bubble in the American housing industry had gone global.

The Federal Government to the Rescue?

Just as the United States slid into a financial crisis, Americans were choosing a new commander in chief. The new president, Barack Obama, was faced with the decision of how to fix the economy. Should the federal government stay out of economic policy, as some economists suggested, and let market forces correct the problems? Or should the government attempt to reverse the economic freefall and protect its citizens from the harshest effects of the recession?

Part of the reason people voted for President Obama was because he had expressed a strong determination to be active and aggressive in his attempts to revive the economy. On January 28, 2009, the House of Representatives approved an $819 billion economic recovery plan. It would take time for the money to be fully distributed. It would take even longer to tell if the spending plan worked and helped reverse the recession.

There will always be ups and downs in the stock market. There will be winners and losers. The same people who are winners one day can become losers the next day. People who once thought they lost it all in the stock market can suddenly find that they have made a fortune. The same risk that drives some people away from this kind of money investment can attract other people.

The stock market is not always a hair-raising roller coaster ride, however, characterized by dramatic peaks and stomach-churning drops. The general trend of the stock market over the last two hundred years and more has been a solid and steady upward swing, with occasional—and occasionally steep—setbacks. Over time most investors see a healthy return on their investments, usually far outstripping the interest that money can earn in a savings account. As long as investors are aware of the risks, research their investments, invest only a portion of their savings, and spread their money around many different companies to minimize the chance of sudden huge losses, the stock market can be a fairly reliable and effective way to increase personal wealth, support American corporations, and keep the economy humming.

asking price The price at which someone is offering to sell a stock.

bear market A market in which stock prices fall for an extended period of time, specifically 20 percent or more over at least a two-month period.

bid price The price that someone is offering to buy a stock for.

bull market A market in which stock prices consistently increase over time.

credit An agreement in which someone buys something now and promises to pay for it later.

dividend A share of profits paid by a company to its shareholders.

Dow Jones Industrial Average An index consisting of thirty industrial companies whose stock performances provide a standard measure of the stock market's value.

economic cycle A series of changes in the overall business activities in a country that occurs over and over.

exchange A company that provides facilities to trade stocks, bonds, mutual funds, or other types of investments.

index A group of companies whose stock represents the typical performance of a market or sector.

investing The risking of money and time to get more money in return.

loan A sum of money borrowed for a certain amount of time.

mutual fund An investment run by professionals in which people pool their money to buy stocks, bonds, and other items.

profits The realized earnings by the investor after a stock is sold.

quote The price of a stock at any given time.

return on investment The amount of money you make from an investment, in dollars or as a percentage.

short selling The act of investing in a stock based on the belief that its price will drop.

split The dividing of a stock, usually in half, in order to lower the price, making it more attractive to investors.

stock An investment in the ownership of a company.

Federal Deposit Insurance Corporation (FDIC)
Consumer Response Center
2345 Grand Boulevard, Suite 100
Kansas City, MO 64108-2638
(800) 378-9581
Web site: http://www.fdic.gov
The FDIC insures bank accounts. Its Web site also provides a variety
of information related to banking and the state of banks.

Fidelity Investments
82 Devonshire Street
Boston, MA 02109
(800) 544-6666
Web site: http://www.fidelity.com
The number one U.S. provider of retirement accounts, Fidelity
Investments provides information on retirement and non-
retirement investing. Its Web site provides the latest news and
real-time quotes.

House Financial Services Committee
2129 Rayburn House Office Building
Washington, DC 20515
(202) 225-4247
Web site: http://financialservices.house.gov
This committee is responsible for dealing with financial issues and
bills. It is possible to view hearings over the Internet and obtain
information on various bills that have been passed and are under
consideration and their potential effects on the economy.

Investment Industry Regulatory Organization of Canada
121 King Street West, Suite 1600
Toronto, ON M5H 3T9

Canada
(416) 364-6133
Web site: http://www.iiroc.ca
This is the organization that regulates stock transactions in Canada
and provides information about stock rules.

New York Stock Exchange (NYSE)
11 Wall Street
New York, NY 10005
(212) 656-3000
Web site: http://www.nyse.com/home.html
The NYSE is the most well-known stock exchange in the United States.
Its Web site provides a variety of information related to stocks.

Security Investment Protection Corporation
805 Fifteenth Street NW, Suite 800
Washington, DC 20005
(202) 371-8300
Web site: http://www.sipc.org/contact.cfm
This organization insures investment accounts. It also provides
information on protections for investment accounts.

U.S. Department of the Treasury
1500 Pennsylvania Avenue SW
Washington, DC 20220
(202) 622-2000
Web site: http://www.ustreas.gov
The Treasury Department is responsible for monitoring and managing the overall state of the U.S. economy. Its Web site includes
the latest information on financial markets, as well as information on the various types of bonds issued by the federal
government.

U.S. Securities and Exchange Commission (SEC)
100 F Street NE
Washington, DC 20549
(202) 942-8080
Web site: http://www.sec.gov
The SEC is the organization that regulates investing in the United
States. It provides educational written publications and a variety
of useful calculators on its Web site.

Vanguard
455 Devon Park Drive
Wayne, PA 19087
(877) 662-7447
Web site: http://www.vanguard.com
Vanguard pioneered the index mutual fund, which contains the
same companies found in major indexes. Its Web site provides
market news.

Web Sites

Due to the changing nature of Internet links, Rosen Publishing has
developed an online list of Web sites related to the subject of this
book. This site is updated regularly. Please use this link to access
the list:

http://www.rosenlinks.com/dol/stock

Brancato, Robin. *Money: The Ultimate Teen Guide*. Blue Ridge Summit, PA: The Scarecrow Press, 2006.

Cauvier, Denis, and Alan Lysaght. *The ABCs of Making Money 4 Teens*. Ogdensburg, NY: Wealth Solutions Press, 2005.

Collins, Robyn, and Kimberly Spinks Burleson. *Prepare to Be a Teen Millionaire*. Deerfield Beach, FL: HCI, 2008.

Cramer, Jim. *Stay Mad for Life: Get Rich, Stay Rich* (Make Your Kids Even Richer). New York, NY: Simon & Schuster, 2007.

Denega, Danielle. *Smart Money: How to Manage Your Cash*. London, England: Franklin Watts, 2008.

Drobot, Eve. *Money, Money, Money: Where It Comes From, How to Save It, Spend It and Make It*. Toronto, ON: Maple Tree Press, Inc., 2004.

Foster, Chad. *Financial Literacy for Teens*. Conyers, GA: Rising Books, 2004.

Hollander, Barbara. *Managing Money*. Chicago, IL: Heineman, 2008.

Holmberg, Joshua, and David Bruzzese. *The Teen's Guide to Personal Finance: Basic Concepts in Personal Finance That Every Teen Should Know*. Littleton, CO: iUniverse, 2008.

Raynolds, Laura. *Fair Trade: The Challenges of Transforming Globalization*. New York, NY: Policy Library, 2007.

Silver, Don. *High School Money Book*. Los Angeles, CA: Adams-Hall Publishing, 2007.

Stahl, Mike. *Early to Rise: A Young Adult's Guide to Investing and Financial Decisions That Can Shape Your Life*. Los Angeles, CA: Silver Lake Publishing, 2005.

Steger, Manfred B. *Globalization: A Very Short Introduction*. Rev. ed. New York, NY: Oxford University Press, 2009.

Wuorio, Jeffrey J. *The Complete Idiot's Guide to Retirement Planning*. Indianapolis, IN: Alpha, 2007.

INDEX

About the Authors

Charles North is a writer living in New Jersey.

Charles Caes is a writer living in Virginia.

Photo Credits

Cover, pp. 6, 17, 30, 37, 47 Steven Puetzer/Photonica/ Getty Images; interior graphics © www.istockphoto.com/ mecalega; page number background istockphoto/Thinkstock; p. 7 Stan Honda/AFP/Getty Images; pp. 10–11 MN Chan/Getty Images News/Getty Images; pp. 12–13, 24–25 Bloomberg/ Bloomberg via Getty Images; p. 14 William Thomas Cain/ Getty Images News/Getty Images; pp. 18–19 Lars Baron/ Getty Images News/Getty Images; p. 20 Superstock/Getty Images; pp. 26–27 Miguel Villagran/Getty Images News/Getty Images; pp. 31, 38–39, 41, 44–45, 52 Shutterstock; p. 33 © www.istockphoto.com/Tom Fewster; p. 35 David Woodfall/ Photographer's Choice/Getty Images; pp. 42–43 © www. istockphoto.com/Eyeidea®; p. 48 Paul J. Richards/AFP/Getty Images; pp. 50–51 Mario Tama/Getty Images News/Getty Images; p. 54 Brendan Smialowski/Getty Images News/Getty Images.

Editor: Nicholas Croce; Designer: Nicole Russo;
Photo Researcher: Marty Levick